AT EVERY WEDDING
SOMEONE STAYS HOME

Poems by Dannye Romine Powell

THE UNIVERSITY OF ARKANSAS PRESS

FAYETTEVILLE   1994

D1472985

Copyright © 1994 by Dannye Romine Powell
All rights reserved
Manufactured in the United States of America
98   97   96   95   94   5   4   3   2   1

Designed by Gail Carter

The paper used in this publication meets the minimum
requirements of the American National Standard for
Permanence of Paper for Printed Library Materials
Z19.48-1984.   ⊜

Library of Congress Cataloging-in-Publication Data
Powell, Dannye Romine.
    At every wedding someone stays home : poems /
by Dannye Romine Powell.
        p. cm. — (Arkansas poetry award series)
        ISBN 1-55728-315-X. — ISBN 1-55728-316-8 (pbk.)
        I. Title. II. Series.
PS3566.08267A93   1994
811'.54—dc20   93-38795
                                                   CIP

For Lew

ACKNOWLEDGMENTS

Grateful acknowledgment is made to the editors of the following publications, in which the following poems first appeared, some in earlier versions: *Beloit Poetry Journal* ("Mary Lamb: The Murder"); *Birmingham Poetry Review* ("In a New Country"); *The Cairn* ("Why I Yell at My Husband"); *Calliope* ("At Every Wedding Someone Stays Home" and "Let's Say We Haven't Seen Each Other Since Ninth Grade . . ."); *Crazyhorse* ("The Day You Died I Thought It Would Be As Hard . . ." and "Almost Fifty"); *Folio* ("Sisters"); *Georgia Journal* ("I Am My Mother, Primping," "I Like To Imagine We Are Starting Over" and "The Sorrow in Schoolyards"); *Georgia Review* ("My Mother, Becoming a Widow"); *Gettysburg Review* ("The Absence of Bounty" and "Hope, Which for Years Kept Resurfacing, Now Crumbles"); *The Little Magazine* ("Geography Lesson" and "Now Adam"); *Northeast* ("Found Poem"); *Northwest Review* ("Sorrow, Looking Like Abraham Lincoln, Keeps Knocking on My Back Door"); *Paris Review* ("In the Periodical Room"); *Poem* ("Why I'm against Liposuction" and "On What Would Have Been Our Twenty-Fifth Anniversary"); *Poets On: Loss* ("Three Reasons to Stop Banging Your Head against the Wall"); *Prairie Schooner* ("Before the News"); *River Styx* ("Yard Sale: Charlotte, N.C."); *Shenandoah* ("Mothers, Attend the Women Your Sons Marry"); *South Carolina Review* ("Primer on Digging"); *Southern Poetry Review* ("Shredding the Letters"); *Southern Review* ("My Father and Johnny"); *Sycamore Review* ("At Morrow Mountain").

"In the Periodical Room" and "Now Adam" appeared in *Reading Rooms: America's Foremost Writers Celebrate Our Public Libraries with Stories, Memoirs, Essays, and Poems*, edited by Susan Allen Toth and John Coughlan. Foreword by Daniel J. Boorstin. Doubleday. 1991.

"At Every Wedding Someone Stays Home" "My Mother, Becoming A Widow," "Sorrow, Looking Like Abraham Lincoln," and "Mary Lamb" appeared in *Trapping Time Between the Branches: An Anthology from Charlotte's Poets,* edited by Don Carroll and Frye Gaillard. Public Library of Charlotte and Mecklenburg County, 1993.

"Primer on Digging" appeared in *Contemporary Poetry of North Carolina,* edited by Guy Owen and Mary C. Williams. John F. Blair Publishers, 1977.

"Almost Fifty" will appear in *Each in Her Own Way,* edited by Elizabeth Clamen. Queen of Swords Press, 1994.

"In the Periodical Room" appeared in *The Imaginative Spirit: Literary Heritage of Charlotte and Mecklenburg County,* edited by Mary Norton Kratt. Public Library of Charlotte and Mecklenburg County, 1988.

CONTENTS

SWEEPING THIS ONE ROOM

THICK AS FIG LEAVES

THE MAD ARE FULL OF THEMSELVES

SWEEPING THIS
ONE ROOM

MEMORY

I know where you sit:
in the back rows
of old theatres,
the kind with stenciled stars
in the navy-blue ceiling.
The films you watch
are spliced, scratched,
the actors dead or forgotten.
On days like this—
cold, the sky overloaded—
you could be someone's uncle,
huddled in your overcoat,
eating popcorn, feet propped
on the seat ahead.

SISTERS

I reach high
on the closet shelf
and find your sister's braid
snipped sixty years ago,
coiled in a hat box,
wrapped in tissue,
still glistening
and blond.

"We can toss that,"
you say, and I remember
all the reasons you gave
when I was growing up
why my hair
should be kept short.
You weren't up to
having a daughter
with long hair, you'd say,
recalling the trouble
your sister's hair
caused your mother.

Your sister's hair
was so heavy, you'd say,
your poor mother
had to get on her knees,

bend over the tub
to hold that hair up
while you soaped
the cloth
so she could scrub
her neck.

That hair
was so long,
you told me,
so thick,
your mother insisted
your sister sit on it
when she played
the piano or guests
might be distracted
by its shimmering
and miss the music.

I watch you
put the lid back
on that box
and I can see you
as a child
leaning against the piano.
Your sister's long fingers

are flying, her hair trembles
to the bench. Your hand
is on your narrow hip,
the thing you cannot name
a tight, dark plait
at your neck.

THE ABSENCE OF BOUNTY

A small crowd gathers
in my mother's living room.
They're all there, she says.
Her sister Frances, her cousin
Vivien, even her nephew Leonard
back from the dead. My mother
goes into the kitchen
and discovers her cupboards
are bare. This is a dream
my mother dreams repeatedly,
no matter where she lives.
When she tells it we never consider
the guests leaning their elbows
on the arms of the sofa, waiting.
They could be parched
or starved for all we care.
What matters is the air
of those bare cupboards, the emptiness
scurrying like ants, corner
to corner. Remember: This
is my mother's dream. But watch
how she pulls me in, the twin taps
of our fingers on the counter tops,
despair stacking up between us like tins.

MY FATHER AND JOHNNY

Miami, Florida. February, 1950

This is the month that keeps returning, Miami sky
cool as silk. Hibiscus and frangipani in bloom,
lawns crisp as new twenties. Florence and Johnny—
my aunt and uncle from Savannah—are here for their
two-week visit. My parents play hooky from routine,
making me feel, at nine, like the only adult in the family.

As I walk to school, I like to imagine the two men,
driving in the Keys over the Seven Mile Bridge, Johnny
cracking jokes, my father smoking Luckies,
slapping his khaki leg. Every few miles
Johnny rolls down the window and spits
toward the ocean, wipes his mouth with the back of his
        hand
as if he'd swallowed something thick and delicious.

At school, we line up by the cherry hedge, high
as our heads, and march to our rooms. I picture my
        father
and Johnny unloading their tackle at Spec's Boat Rentals
near Six Mile Reef. My father almost forgets, goes back
to the car for the lunch my mother packed: roast beef
sandwiches, celery sticks, a teaspoon of salt folded
in waxed paper, cookies. Enough for two.

I slide into my desk and know my mother's high heel
slippers are clicking across the Florida room floor.

If they're going shopping, my mother wants to get
    moving.
As my teacher writes today's date on the board,
I can see Florence, who's never rushed in her life,
examining her beautiful plump breasts in the mirror.
She is not checking for lumps. She is just checking.

You may be imagining that now the PA system
crackles to life and the principal calls me
to the office to say there's been an accident.
But this is the fifties. One balmy day tacks
into another. Palm trees. Brief afternoon showers.
Even my mother's father, whom I call Papa,
is still alive in Social Circle, Georgia.

My father and Johnny are home before dusk,
exhausted, they say, smelling of mullet
and sweat. From the porch, I watch them clean
and filet the snapper and grouper, Johnny hosing
blood and scales. Inside, Florence spreads cards
on the table for solitaire. My mother opens a drawer,
looking for the white linen cloth.

Then it's February, 1992, a day as mild and blue
as any February morning in Miami, the temperature
near seventy. Johnny's been dead for years. Florence

lives with her daughter on Sullivan's Island. My children
are grown, one married. In Covington, Georgia, my
        father
lies on his side, dying of cancer. My mother tempts him
with food—milk shakes, rice, cold tomato soup.

He says he dreams he is driving in the Keys,
opening his windows on the Seven Mile Bridge, salt air
stinging his lungs. Every Sunday I visit,
holding his hand longer and longer, believing
I'm seeing him alive for the last time. Driving home
through the Carolinas, it all sails back—
silk sky, an expanse of water, the enormity of blue.

GEOGRAPHY LESSON

Those magnificent parks
in Louisville, Kentucky,
she often says, and all you remember
is that awful worm you found
crawling in your corn. Mother,
you are wrong. I remember far more
of that war-time summer I was three.
The room at the head of the stair
where warm air churned
warm air and you napped
the wrinkled afternoon while I strolled
my teddy bear around the floral floor.

That cucumber you were scoring
when you told my father
to take his daughter to the movies. After all,
you said above my head, flicking peelings
into the sink, your father prefers blondes.
Later, the red tip of his cigarette burning,
burning a hole in the dark
beneath the dark. I remember
more of Louisville, Kentucky, Mother,
but I smile and nod when you mention
the worm.

MY MOTHER, BECOMING A WIDOW

Pines
scraping
a swollen moon.
The hairline crack
in the basement window.
Cold tines of a fork
against dry lips.
Ice collecting
on the pond
near the field
yarrow lit last June.

THE DAY YOU DIED I THOUGHT IT WOULD BE AS HARD AS HAVING TO HAUL ALL MY FURNITURE INTO THE BACKYARD THEN SWEEP UP IN LESS THAN AN HOUR

For my father

But it was only like dusting.
I went home and picked up an old soft cloth
and started caressing the table tops,
taking pains, like company's coming,
lifting the tinted photo
of your mother at sixteen, the one
in the small oval frame,
her blue eyes dreaming past us both.
That picture and the brass bell. Dusting
under, not around, everything. Easy.

Now weeks later, I see I've only begun.
This morning, I started on the dining room,
dragged the cane-bottomed chairs out,
wrapped the table leaves,
each one heavy as marble, propped them
against the oak. There's still an attic full,
plus beds and linens and books.
This afternoon, I'll tackle
the Victorian hutch. Tomorrow,
after sleep, I'll roll up the woven rug.
Something tells me it's full of sand.
I'm beginning to see I could be sweeping
this one room for months. Sweeping
this one room. This one room. Empty and dumb.

THICK AS FIG LEAVES

HOW I STILL THINK OF YOU

Like a tropical rain
the kind you see coming for blocks
mid–afternoons, carrying the odor
of the next town over,
the kind mothers rouse their children
from naps to see, gathering them
at the door to watch its silvery pelt
before it moves on out to sea,
the street already dry now
where the girls playing hopscotch
stand soaked, those girls who saw it coming,
who knew they had time to run inside
but stood there, lulled by its soft canter,
its thin curtain of mercury,
the loose, high sheen, those girls
who stand there yet, yellow chalk crumbling
in their small, tight hands.

YOU ARE SITTING ACROSS FROM ME
AT THE KITCHEN TABLE IN FULL SUN

And I am studying
your lips
which are no longer
lean and fearsome lips
crossed by a shadow
but softer more domestic
lips. I sit transfixed
watching you spoon in cereal
and milk, missing the danger
of your old risky lips.
So I have to ask myself
if I can still look at you
and feel bliss. I can,
yes, but I admit
it's more like the bliss
I feel for myself
sitting across from you
here in full sun
spooning in cereal and milk.

FOR MY HUSBAND,
WHO PREFERS SEX TO GARDENING

June and all I want
is to linger in my loamy beds,
dig, turn my soil. I could weed
all night, ogle my sprengeria ferns,
my thread-leaf coreopsis
tossing stars, the frilled and stewy tansy,
the crowd of black-eyed Susans
yearning toward the sun.

Inside, my husband has finished
the evening news. I hear him roaming,
opening, closing cabinets, turning on
and off the faucets. I know he's fed.
There's ice cream in the freezer.

Now he's tapping on the pane
above the bed where I'm troweling
on my knees. I dig beneath
a dandelion, ease its length
to light. I can ignore him
until he thrusts a window up. "Come
inside, my peach, my plum," he whispers
against the screen. "You are my dirt,
my loam, my little piece of earth.
And let me tell you something
you may not know, sweetheart: Inside,
inside it's growing fiercely dark."

I LIKE TO IMAGINE WE ARE STARTING OVER

A green farmhouse,
bare floors,
deep porch
facing west.
You are hauling
in wood.
I am hanging cups
on hooks. Soon
I will set
the table
for supper.
White plates,
blue napkins,
our good silver.
Out the window
a swell of crickets
and pine. Deep
in my pocket
columbine seed.

AT MORROW MOUNTAIN

On a slope of this mountain,
everything seems so simple.
Out my window, birch, oak, poplar,
the crazy mosaic of pine bark.
I eat when I'm hungry—bread,
cheese, peaches. Wind whorls somewhere
at the tops of trees. Are you miles away
or thousands of miles away? Last night,
a family of raccoons nudged
at my screen. Deer, necks angling
to the ground, stray close
to the porch, bolt at the rustle
of paper. I surprise myself
alone. I'm bolder than I thought.
Yesterday, I hiked miles through woods,
then swamps, followed the curve
of the Pee Dee River, climbed boulders
to see the waterfall. In a few hours
I'll pack up, head back. I'll miss
the silence here, the scatter
of light on leaves, appearing,
disappearing. A warning: When
I arrive, don't gauge my presence
by my distance. Reach for me.

LET'S SAY WE HAVEN'T SEEN EACH OTHER SINCE NINTH GRADE AND WE MEET AS ADULTS AT A WELCOME CENTER IN SOUTHSIDE VIRGINIA

And we begin to kiss
the way we used to kiss
before you moved
with your parents
to Michigan: after school
out by the chain link fence
near the basketball court
on the sea wall
by the bay
in the church parking lot
after choir practice
flat on our backs
in the grass
at slumber parties
before the boys had to leave
or on the beach at Matheson Hammock
when your sister
would drive us
then go off somewhere else
to work on her tan.

It takes us a few seconds
to adjust our arms
because you are taller now
but it all comes back
how we used to take turns

catching our breath,
where your right ear lobe
is fleshy, how your collar smells
of heather, which tooth protrudes,
the scar on your chin
that used to be higher.

I can smell the cream
of gardenias in the purple bowl
on our homeroom teacher's desk,
I can even remember her name—
Mrs. Bleier—and I can see the dance
of mimosas in the patio after lunch,
the hair on my arms standing up
when the sun slid behind clouds
and how you kept them up
until the sun eased out again,
the choir singing deep
and wide, deep and wide,
there is a fountain flowing
deep and wide
and how I always thought of you
instead of Jesus when we sang
I've got joy joy joy joy
down in my heart, down in my heart,
the way I do now, kissing you

at a Welcome Center
just over the state line
in Southside Virginia.

WHEN SHE HEARS THE ONE SHE LOVES AND CANNOT HAVE, SAY A WORD AS BEAUTIFUL AND TENDER AS THE WORD *ARBOR*

Pebbles stutter
to the surface
of earth, collapse
in her garden, flattening
pansies and thrift.
All day she clicks
the smooth stones
into her apron,
makes tidy mounds
behind the hedge. *Arbor,*
he says. Robins topple
from trees, beaks open,
eyes cold beads.
She plucks their feathers
for pillows, hungry
for sleep. *Arbor,*
he says. Miles away
wheat shudders
in the field. She walks
all night to float
on its ocean.
If she covers her ears
with shells
she believes the sky
won't open,
believes hail

won't clatter
across her lids,
believes she'll never wake
to the flat, white ache of hope.

SHREDDING THE LETTERS

I am shredding your letters
like lettuce:
the Taoist sayings,
quotes from the Poetics.
Watch how they drift.
Watch how they dot the river
like popcorn.
They ascend to the headwaters
and spawn like salmon.
Their eggs hatch into pyramids.

From my window I watch tourists
climb the steep steps
to worship the sun.
I watch them sit down
to have heart attacks.
Step by step
the pyramids descend
into the river.
No one knows what happened
to the people
or their souvenirs.
The tips of the pyramids
are barely visible in the water.

A few minutes later,

a bridge opens over the river
and a ship glides through.
People wait in their cars
for the bridge to go down.
They smoke cigarettes
to make the time pass.
They do not know the ship's hull
will be rent. The event
has not yet made headlines.

I only shredded the letters
in order to clear my throat.
Later I realize
it may have been safer to burn them.

I AM MY MOTHER, PRIMPING

She had a certain way
of raising her chin
then angling her face
side to side. That final
glancing appraisal
before she lifted
the hand mirror
then reversed herself
to inspect the back
held me faster
than the woolen violets
that swept her hair
in place, the gold earrings
shaped like roses.

My husband asks why
I hold my mouth
a certain way
when I comb my hair.
Which way? I ask, annoyed.
Doesn't he know
in this reflection
my lips are fuller,
cheekbones bolder.
Above the ear,
a cluster of purple spring.

WHY I YELL AT MY HUSBAND

My father loved danger
even more than he hated waiting
so when the horn blew
on the Rickenbacker Causeway
to alert drivers
the bridge was going up
he would bolt across
seconds after the other cars
had stopped. One Sunday
when I was six, we felt the click
of the bridge opening
beneath our wheels. My mother
slammed her feet to the floor
but never opened her mouth.
I wanted her to shout don't ever
do that again, to yell
how we could've been tossed
over the railing into the ocean
or been caught by our wheels
on the edge of the bridge
to dangle forever high over Miami.
She never did. Instead, she got a headache.
Back home, she undressed,
adjusted the Venetian blinds
so the last of the sun

fell to the carpet in strips. Later,
when I tiptoed past her room,
those old brackish waves spumed against my heart.

ON WHAT WOULD HAVE BEEN OUR
TWENTY-FIFTH ANNIVERSARY

I never thought of silver
but I tried every other color.
In Hillsborough, I turned
a wicker baby carriage
into a flutter of buttercup
yellow. In Durham,
I was bolder, splashed
flat apricot
on the refrigerator,
told the landlady
it would wash off, transformed
a cardboard wardrobe
with six coats of blue.
In Raleigh, when your aunt died,
I antiqued her gate-leg table
mint-green, sprayed
her wooden curtain rings
red for Christmas. In the spring,
our filing cabinets gleamed
the color of Granny Smith
apples. Later, we started
collecting a few pieces too good
to paint. There was nothing
to do but turn to the outdoors:
fences, shutters, porches.

The day you said you were leaving
I could hear paint peeling
all over the state.

NOW ADAM

You can borrow *Adam* from the public library
for six weeks at a time, no renewals.
I tried it as an experiment, lugged him
home, settled his lusty weight
upon my bureau. He didn't turn his head
when I undressed, but kept his chin
solidly pressed into his shoulder. Relax,
I whispered in his plastered ear.
The world's undone, we all fell long ago.
He didn't flinch. It's not your rib
I'm after, I insisted, just some sign
you're aware I exist. He didn't bat
a lash, but gazed, gazed his steady gaze
out my window.

Next I offered apples, first whole,
then sliced, finally pan fried with cinnamon.
He didn't give a tendon. Out of wiles,
I told him straight: Look, Adam, if you want
the cubic truth, unless you can take
some affirmative action, you're out of fashion,
a mass of idle weight. He didn't budge,
but gazed, gazed his steady gaze
until dusk fell thick as fig leaves
about our naked feet.

THE MAD ARE FULL
OF THEMSELVES

DON'T PRETEND TO BE SURPRISED

A teenager in Rochester decides to say
she found the newborn in a cardboard box
on top of the garbage.

We women are no strangers to stealth,
that old asthmatic who fills our back rooms
with longing and a hacking cough.
We know pleasure and peril
knock on the same door. We're not fooled,
but we keep on fooling.

Watch the girl's mother
when the girl appears in the doorway
holding her naked baby in a towel.
The mother is pouring cereal
into her husband's porcelain bowl,
her own secrets jingling like trinkets.

The girl says she found the baby
out back. Does the mother doubt her daughter,
this child in the pink fleecy robe,
eyes stitched wide? Not for a moment.

She reaches for the baby, holds it close.
If, in the sleeping face, she sees her own,

she doesn't let on. The baby lies snug in her towel, a plump bundle mother and daughter will trade back and forth, back and forth for all time.

YARD SALE: CHARLOTTE, N.C.

"Pareja is a town where the people are full of ideas."
—Amilo Jose Cela

The balding man
is selling out, emptying
the frame house where he's lived
all his life with his mother.
My husband wants to inspect
everything. He moves from table to table:
baseball cards in plastic
holders, portable sewing machine,
commemorative plates, one thumb
hooked in his back pocket.

I study two cedar trees
at the entrance to the yard, one
on either side of the steps, so wide
they meet in the middle, blocking
the walk. At the base of the trees,
shade pools in a space just tall enough
for a child to idle away
summer mornings playing house.

When the man wanders over
I want to ask how he could allow
the cedars to grow so thick.
Instead, I say, What a perfect place
for a playhouse. Instantly, we are friends.
He points to the top of the trees, showing me

where he had planned to sculpt a Moorish arch
so visitors climbing the steps
might imagine they smelled the sea.

As a child, I loved these cedars,
he says, lifting a branch
and stroking it. I could throw myself
into them and they would support
my whole weight. Then, before my eyes,
this grown man, this grown, balding man,
hurls himself into one of the trees,
showing me his old game. He straightens,
smiles. The branches bob, subside.
He brushes flecks of cedar from his face
while around us morning deepens into Moroccan blue.

MOTHERS, ATTEND THE WOMEN
YOUR SONS MARRY

One will choose
your fairer self,
the one you believe
you are. Each spring
she bends on her knee
to sow seeds of fennel
and lemon verbena.
Her white cotton gowns
are embroidered by hand.
When she spins, light nestles
in her hair. Her life
is a butterfly stroke
through clear water.

The other turns
this way and that.
The hem of her robe
drags the floor
and collects dust.
The curve of her spine
dismays you. Her potatoes
mold in the basement.
Her meat sticks
to the pan.
Her way in the world
is sand in your shoes.

Bend your hearts
to these young Gretels.
They will lead you
into the thicket
and out. You are the one
who built the sweet house
of raisins and bread,
plumped the pillows
on the little white beds.
And you are the one
who squints through the window,
offers crayfish shells
to the hungry
and hides the venison.

PRIMER ON DIGGING

*"Memory is the characteristic art form of those who have
just decided to die and those who have just decided to live."*
—Daniel Stern, *The Suicide Academy*

Listen: When you dig
in the garden
expect to be bitten.
Those fish heads you buried
last spring endure beyond seasons,
breeding their own subtleties.
Your fingers will encounter
the slow growth of moss,
the spasms of slugs
recoiling from salt.
Go farther: One mild earthworm
is not sufficient to measure the world.
Hard by the brick wall
the roly-poly unfurls,
a bolus of damp memory
assaulting your nostrils.
Wait. Don't reach for the spade.
You must touch the white root
with your fingers, follow
its search for cool water.
Now that your hands are submerged
notice how the dark treasures
quicken like dreams
beneath your swollen fingertips.

BEFORE THE NEWS

Never mind what you are doing
when the telephone rings.
What matters are those moments before:
the instant the car skids
around the curve, its headlights
plowing the dark. Or the second
he turns the gun into his own mouth.
You might be drawing a bath,
sprinkling the water with crystals,
or bending over your toenails
painting them pink,
your hair brushing your cheeks
like wings. Maybe
you're sealing a letter
to your cousin or opening the oven
to test the bread. You believe
you have time to wander outside
to water the plants. Your hand
is on the knob, your foot
on the step. You are lifting
your face to the sky, your faith
in the moment about to explode
around you like poppies.

THE SORROW IN SCHOOLYARDS

All day you play
at forgetting
whether the train
is to Dallas
or Atlanta,
whether the surgery
will be major or minor.
The notes
giving you permission
you do not want
are stones
in your pockets
and your sorrow swarms
around you like wasps.
You are the ones
who spill your milk,
chew the ends
of pencils.
You are the ones
who open your math books
and weep
at the sight of fractions.

WHY I'M AGAINST LIPOSUCTION

Oh to be surplus.
To bask in rolls of fat,
to be fishes and loaves
after he blessed them,
to feed nations
in one sitting.
To love the words
portly and *stout*,
to introduce them
to your neighbors
and watch them disrobe.
To hear your soul singing
with a swollen joy.
To roll over
and meet yourself coming.
To clasp hands
and be more than you thought.

IN THE PERIODICAL ROOM

At the next table
a woman in patent shoes,
blue summer shift
flips through *House Beautiful*.
On her arm the flat oval
of a smallpox vaccination
gleams like egg yolk.
I feel it is my duty
to reduce her age.
First I tuck her several chins
into her neck,
smooth the fan of wrinkles
from her cheek,
prune all flesh
so bones protrude.
At last she is thirteen,
wears middy blouse
and pleated navy skirt.
Later she will play croquet
on her grandfather's lawn.
A balding man in nylon socks,
khaki shorts
approaches her table.
He smoothes the space
between his tufts of gray,
checks his watch.

He told his wife
to meet him here
at exactly half past three.
Now all he can find
is this ridiculous girl
swinging her legs,
licking a peppermint stick.

MARY LAMB: THE MURDER

> *On Sept. 22, 1796, Charles Lamb came home from*
> *work to find his sister, Mary, 33, holding a bloody*
> *knife over their mother's dead body. The next day,*
> *a jury returned a verdict of Lunacy.*

I remember a swift beveling
at the rim of my mind, motes
flying, then nothing. Brother Charles
is shy on his visits to the asylum. Doctor says
Charles found me, knife in hand, Mother
splotched and slumped. That morning,
Coleridge's post had arrived with news
of their first-born son. As I straightened
the bed sheets, Sarah's form swam up. She was holding
the tiny boy, her breasts sweet with milk
and sudden flesh. Better air these linens,
I thought. Mother had been sleeping with me
for weeks. Easier to tend her, she said. Still,
I missed the soft contours of solitary dreaming.

I had every intention
of sending Sarah greetings
that morning, but Father called, demanded
I wipe his nose, refill his pipe. Aunt Hetty begged
for me to read the Scriptures aloud. Her sight
is gone, yet she insists on books. She nods, wakes,
wants someone, usually me, to read the passage
open in her lap. I can forgive
anything. Mother's attentions to John
and Charles. The times I've tried

to hold her hand or kiss her hair
and she's pulled back or somehow twisted.

One day, about two weeks ago, she knew
as well as I the boy had brought fresh cod
that morning. Still, at tea, "What's this?"
She sniffed her soup. "Mother,"
I said, "you know it's cod. You saw the boy."
She shoved her bowl. "Not fit,"
she said, then sat picking at her bread.

Hourly, I go over each event.
Rose, my apprentice, came late
that day. We'd never finish all the cloaks
on order, even if we stitched our fingers
to the quick. I longed to sew
through tea, but what if Charles burst in,
starved? He might pace or, worse, begin
to stammer. We put aside our work, went to lay
the table. I handed Rose clean spoons.
She dropped one. I bit my tongue. A knife
went clattering. Who's hurling silverware?
Who's shrieking? *Mother?* For God's sake, stop! *Stop!*

"Hush, Sister," says Charles. "Don't
think." Here in the asylum, I can go for days,

then the screams return. When I wake
to the mad cawing all around, I am not afraid.
Mother will keep me safe. Her spirit hovers near
the bed. "Sleep, Mary," she whispers
soft. "When you wake, love your life. I'll see you
in heaven." She never twists. She never pulls away.

SORROW, LOOKING LIKE ABRAHAM LINCOLN, KEEPS KNOCKING ON MY BACK DOOR

I'm soaking my hands deep in dishwater
when I see him angling across the backyards,
ducking under clotheslines, headed
my way again. It's been six months
since they found my little one dead,
curled under the seat
of the crushed school bus.
That was me they wrote about
in the paper. They said

I wanted to pack dirt
into my mouth. I wanted to sink my face
into the ground. But the screams tore out
and nothing would stop them.

The wreck happened in May,
June before I got my breath.
It was like he knew it. A knock
on my back door. Believe it or not,
he was wearing a stovepipe hat. He leaned
against the railing, holding a wicker basket.
I thought of muffins, could almost smell
them. Blueberry. He held the basket up.
I pulled back the white linen napkin,
a big one, the kind they used to use
on trains. What's in there? Air. Nothing
but air. I've never seen a man

with so much dignity
who had so little to give.

A couple of months later,
I'd taken the feather duster
down from the attic. Somehow I thought
if I got something old
I could go into her room,
begin to sort through her things.
I was wrong. I cracked the door
and smelled her smell. It was like
the whiff from a hair brush
when it needs washing. But to me
it was the sweetest smell
on earth. That's when I saw him coming
again, empty-handed. I went down,
noticed his Adam's apple,
something you can't hold against a man,
but it makes them seem so vulnerable.
He wanted money. Look upstairs,
he said. Check your husband's pockets.
I went straight to the cash
in the oatmeal box. Gave him all I had.

School started. That was the worst.
I went to the store, knew it was crazy
but I bought notebook paper,

green and yellow folders. I could see myself,
the woman who had a daughter at home
and the woman who didn't. What
was I doing? I couldn't stop. Bought
a ruler, eraser, shampoo.
There he was when I got back, waiting
on the steps, whittling. I knew
he was hot in that black suit
so I offered iced tea. I want more,
he said, all you've got. I went inside,
hid the school supplies, filled plastic bags
with odds and ends—picture frames,
canned goods, a toaster I'd gotten
as a wedding present. He twisted
the tops of the bags, wrapped
them around those big hands, hobbled
down the steps. I've never seen a man
so sad to be taking another's goods.

Mid-morning, and here I still stand.
Kettle about to whistle, hands tingling,
more alive in this hot water
than the rest of me has felt in months.
As he gets closer, I can see
he's thinner. The sun strikes his hat.
In this weather, it could be made of ice,

the brim about to melt.
He's the most demanding soul
I've ever known. But this time
I'm ready. I've wrapped up all I have left,
put it on the counter by the door.
He's knocking now. I hand him the package.
A glass butter dish and two knives,
each one in bad need of re-silvering.
A slight bow and he's gone. I watch
until he's not more than a speck,
small as the grains of black dirt
someone routed out of my mouth last May.

THREE REASONS TO STOP BANGING YOUR HEAD AGAINST THE WALL

A friend
who counsels families
of neurology patients
tells me head injury victims
sometimes show
a subtle personality change.
They're nicer, she says.
It's as if the impact
rearranged neurons
in a way medicine
hasn't discovered.
Little things
don't bother them.
Their families say
it's as if edginess
had unloaded its rifle.
But, something goes,
she says. Something's
missing. I've noticed it,
too. That silent abduction
of the senses.
They're like pines
with no bark. Fish
without scales. Kings
who no longer rail,
but swallow their tongues
on the way to the feast.

HOPE, WHICH FOR YEARS KEPT
RESURFACING, NOW CRUMBLES

You can dress it in a two-piece,
hand-tailored frock suit
of the best woolen broadcloth,
tie a silk scarf around its neck,
fit its hands in white knit gloves,
bury it in a cast-iron casket
deep in Louisiana soil
and still someone plowing
a sugar cane field a century later
will think he's hit a pipe,
dig it up, stare through the square glass
window until light darkens the face.
Frightened that someone so old
can look so young, he will re-bury
the coffin in soil too shallow, too weightless.
Years later, someone else will stumble
on it, peer through the window
at the skull's lacy cap
and being curious and also rich
will ship the casket off to Washington
where an anthropologist pries
the rusty lid. Finally, it comes to this:
Skull, teeth, ribs, a brown chunk of liver,
silk and broadcloth collapsing damply against bone.

IN A NEW COUNTRY

Aproned, her own girth delights her. It rides
against the board where she kneads dough
for bread for her neighbors
and married daughters. She likes to imagine herself
in wooden shoes, a sturdy Gertrude, calm as cream.
She's grown fond of stoutness,
how it rises from her feet to encase her calves
and thighs. Anchored inside, she finds her own rhythm,
kneading the dough one hundred, two hundred,
sometimes three hundred times or more.
Over the years, she's learned what it takes
for the craters to sigh and subside,
for the silky strength to emerge. She knows
when she pulls, the dough will stretch and give
without tearing. She holds it to the light
and the flecks of bran remind her of freckles
on young skin. She sighs, remembering
the spindly years: empty sills, only the heat rising.

I HAVE KNOWN STAIRS

and banisters
you would never dream
unless you dreamed them with me.

Even marble steps
will melt, flood your feet,
chill your ankles to the marrow.

And landings. No matter
how sound they first appear
will buckle or dissolve.

Railings can betray you, too.
Once a sturdy walnut post
shrank in my hand to a green silk sash,
then the empty sleeve
of a robe my mother once wore.

You never know
when honest pine will ooze
between your fingers
or billow at either end
like parachutes. You could float
to China or drift to Veracruz,
your sole still longing
for a steady, forthright tread.

AT EVERY WEDDING
SOMEONE STAYS HOME

This one sits all morning
beside the picture window,
staring out at the lawn
which in these situations
is always under a sheet of ice,
even in June. The girl is wearing
her quilted robe, gloves,
fur-lined slippers. Still she can't
get warm. Her mother gets hot
just watching her, so she goes out
for groceries, makes a great show
when she returns of rattling
the brown paper bags she saves
to line the bird cage.
Now she is running water,
peeling melons, humming, arranging
daisies. We who are watching
want the mother to quit making noise,
to stop chopping fruit, to leave
the kitchen. We want her to walk
down the hall to the closet
where the wool blankets are stored.
We want her to gather five or six,
the solids, the stripes,
the MacGregor plaids and tuck them
under her daughter's legs, saving one

for her feet and one for her thin shoulders.
Now we want her to heat water for tea,
bring in wood and quick
before her daughter freezes
seal all the windows
against the stray, chill peal of bells.

ALMOST FIFTY

Awake, I never think
of them. Dreaming,
they fill the ocean,
babies in coconut shells.
I wave from the shore.
They smile as they drift
toward me. I lift them cool
and nude from the water,
their sweet limbs all over me.

I wake to the ping
of acorns on the roof,
remember the summer
I was thirteen, rocking
the first baby I'd ever held.
That cheek against my face,
the head's soft bob,
the silent voweling at my ear.

FOUND POEM

Mr. L. T. McKibbon
January 13, 1926.

Dear Mr. Wood:

I am very much surprised at the tone
of your letter of January 9. There's the suggestion
of a sneer running through it, something
I didn't expect from the General Manager.
You seem to have missed the point

of my letter to you. I was not asking
you to make a concession on the price
of another bird simply because the first one
I bought from you froze to death in my absence.
No. I asked you to make a concession

because the bird you sold me as a singer
and guaranteed to be a singer, never sang.
When I would write you this, asking
permission to return him, I would be told
that he would sing and I would be satisfied.

He never sang, and I am not satisfied.
In your last letter, you evaded
altogether this matter of his not singing.
Your establishment may be so large that the loss
of the good will of one customer

in Monroe, Georgia, will not cost you much.
I'd like to point out that it wouldn't
have cost you much to have kept it.
Sneer if you will, Mr. Wood, but I live alone
in my mother's home on a wide,

tree-lined street. Often, in summer,
the shade seeps indoors,
blotting the light. I had hoped, Mr. Wood,
that one of your Golden Opera Singers
might brighten my front parlor with song.

You say you have just received a new shipment
and you feel confident I would be more fortunate
this time. Let me repeat, Mr. Wood, I will not pay
full price for another bird, no matter how golden,
no matter how feathery, the satisfaction.

THE BARNUM & BAILEY OF CRAZINESS

*"One of the tropes, one of the complaints, down the
ages is that the mad have been so full of themselves."*
—*A Social History of Madness*

Did you expect them
to be easy
in their skins?
Gentle
on the sofa?
These are the ones
who offer cruises
on the River Styx,
damp spins
down Finnish tunnels.
They lead you through
thick mangrove swamps, up
a windless Olympus
at dawn. The mad
will leave their hats
on your hall table,
jostle each other and spit
on the rug. But when
they dance barefoot
into town, shaking
their dreams
like tambourines,
you're always waiting
in the cool of the grove,
the first to nod
and lift the goblet.